Things To Do
Before You're

40

Things To Do
Before You're
40

Over 100 Imaginative, Inspirational and
Irresponsible Ideas To Try Before You Grow Up

Michael O'Mara Books Limited

First published in 2006 by
Michael O'Mara Books Limited
9 Lion Yard
Tremadoc Road
London SW4 7NQ

A CIP catalogue record for this book is available from the
British Library.

ISBN (10 digit): 1-84317-204-6
ISBN (13 digit): 978-1-84317-204-8

10 9 8 7 6 5 4 3 2 1

Written by Kate Gribble and J. A. Wines

Designed by www.burville-riley.com

Printed and bound in Great Britain by Cox & Wyman,
Reading, Berks

www.mombooks.com

Introduction

Turning forty is quite a milestone in life. It sounds properly grown-up, after all. Feeling down about the approaching decrepitude? Fear not! Before you reach the big 4-0, grab those last vestiges of youth with both hands and wring them dry. Knuckle down to making the kind of memories that will last you a lifetime. This book will show you how.

Have you ever *flown over your house*? *Travelled to every continent*? *Driven a tractor*? Perhaps not. But work your way through this book, and you'll be challenged to do all three, as well as many other things besides. With suggestions ranging from the inspirational and thought-provoking to the frivolous and fun, *Things To Do Before You're 40* will ensure that those last few years of youth are (mis)spent wisely. Stave off your middle age with a sense of humour, adventure and spirit – and by completing every action-packed proposal contained herein. Dare yourself to make the most of life – and not just because you've got the birthday blues, but because life would be boring if you didn't. Whatever your age, be fearless in finding new ways to inspire yourself. This book is just the beginning . . .

Oh, and Many Happy Returns.

Talk to an older person about their childhood

Many elderly people begin monologues with the cry: 'Ah, when I was young . . .' Have you ever listened to what follows? With your full attention? There are fewer things more fascinating than hearing a first-hand account of a bygone era. If said older person is a member of your family, perhaps a parent or grandparent, you'll gain insights into family roots you never knew existed (better to trip over them now than in therapy). Make an afternoon of it and perhaps *have Tea at the Ritz* with your elderly friend. For really salacious titbits about their teenage years, slip some whisky into their Earl Grey.

Build a snowman

Okay, so depending on where you spent your childhood, you may already have made hundreds of these ice-cool creations. Or maybe snow was such a rarity you can remember each one like an old friend. Whatever the specifics of your snowman CV, it's time to start afresh. If, aged thirty-plus, the prospect of building a snowman in full view of your neighbours fills you with the fear of looking foolish, either *do a tequila slammer* first, or *have a baby* and use your child as a cover.

Reasons to build a snowman:

- It's fun.
- It puts you in touch with your creative side (and is cheaper than *taking an evening class*).
- In the era of global warming, we have to make the most of snowy weather when it comes. Our grandchildren may not have the pleasure of making snowmen (though they will have great all-year tans): take full photographic evidence of your efforts, so that you can share the experience with them in an annual slideshow and hour-long talk they're bound to cherish.
- With adulthood comes a wide-ranging knowledge of your supermarket's fruit-and-veg section. Forget the rest of your neighbourhood's efforts, with their lacklustre show of carrot noses and tangerines: get competitive. A pineapple Mohican, perhaps? Mango buttons on his coat? An avocado makes the perfect Roman nose. Afterwards, blend your snowman's face into a tasty smoothie.

Ask for a pay rise

There once was a time when you got what you were given. That was back in the Victorian era. Even then, however, there were those who pushed the barriers: 'Please, Sir, can I have some more?' Take a leaf out of Oliver Twist's book and ask your boss the same. What have you got to lose? (Okay, your job, but you're unlikely to get the sack for asking a simple question.) Know your own worth at work – if you're confident that you're good at what you do, demand a salary that reflects those high standards.

Some bosses avoid the subject of pay rises like the plague. Ask for an appraisal, instead. At the end of the appraisal, blindside them by asking for a pay rise. Use the evidence in your appraisal to pressurize them into it.

If you're crap at your job, use the carrot-and-stick approach. If they'll give you the carrot of a pay rise, you'll stick at the job. Well, it's worth a try.

If your boss refuses to give you a pay rise, you can always consider *telling them where to shove their job*.

Go on a blind date

Blind dates are nerve-racking, yet potentially thrilling events. Whether you're a veteran on the dating scene or a debutant(e) divorcee, there are some hard-and-fast guidelines to abide by. First, you have to look your best. (This isn't the moment to *make a fashion faux pas*.) The last thing you want is for your date to give you the once-over and walk on by. Second, be recognizable. There's the old carnation-in-the-buttonhole trick, or holding a copy of *The Times* (to make a really good impression, *complete the cryptic crossword* while you're waiting), or simply look a bit desperate and they're bound to pick you out of the crowd.

A friend might be matchmaking, or perhaps you've met this person online or via a dating agency. Whatever the scenario, everyone has the fear that their blind date will be a minger. But there's an equal chance that they'll be a fox. With odds like that, surely it's worth a *gamble*? Let's face it, usually it's either love at first sight or a downright disaster. And there's only one way to find out which . . .

Have a lost weekend

What's the point of getting to forty and being able to remember every single day? (Until your senile dementia kicks in, that is.) Make sure there's at least one weekend remembered solely for the killer hangover on the Monday morning. The weekend will have been the stuff of legend. You won't recall a thing, of course – but if you're unlucky your friends will have documented it for you in gory technicolour detail, perhaps with the kind of photographic evidence that will make you wish you'd never been born, let alone lived four decades. Perhaps this was the time you *spent the night in police cells*? *Became a street performer*? *Had sex in public*? Along the way, as well as losing a weekend, you may well lose an eyebrow, your wallet, dignity, continence or even

 your liberty. As long as you passed out with a smile on your face, the chances are it will have been worth it.

TOP TIPS:

- Drink as though your life depends on it.
- Accept every dare.
- Believe you are invincible.
- Book Monday off work (unless you are a functioning alcoholic).

Run to the top of a hill and shout, 'I am the king of the world!'

Visit an art gallery

It's never too early or too late to acquire an introduction to the art world, but by forty you should at least be familiar with a Turner, a Gainsborough, a Monet, a Picasso, a Goya, and a Dutch master or two, and that's just for starters. Before your fifth decade, you really should  have seen the *Mona Lisa*'s smile (prepare to queue for hours if you haven't), Michelangelo's David and Rodin's Kiss. On the contemporary side, you should have at least a half-formed opinion on Damien Hirst and formaldehyde, and seen for yourself what all the fuss was about with Tracey Emin's bed.

A handful of good galleries to visit includes:

- The National Gallery, Tate Britain, Tate Modern, the National Portrait Gallery, the Royal Academy of Arts and the Hayward Gallery, all in London.
- The Metropolitan Museum of Art in New York City.
- The Uffizi Gallery in Florence.

- The Musée du Louvre, Musée d'Orsay, and Centre Pompidou in Paris.
- The Guggenheim Museum in Bilbao.
- The Museum of Bad Art in Boston.

Retake an exam you failed or did badly in when you were young

---

Become a part of your local community

Do you know the names of your neighbours? If not, why not? In living a life of social exclusion, you're shutting off routes to free babysitters, house-watchers, potential dinner-party guests and even friends. Pop next door today and ask to borrow a cup of sugar. Take the opportunity to check out the décor – be friends with the Joneses, but keep up with them, too.

In ye olde days, local communities used to organize events together. Do the same – host a street party in the summer, or just a general piss-up (nothing bonds like booze). Make more of annual festivities. Go trick or treating. Start up a Neighbourhood Watch scheme, so you can watch each other's backs. Go carol singing at Christmas time (or whenever you need to make a quick buck), and make a note in your diary to attend the local school fête. Take pride in knowing everyone in your block or street.

See a band you've never heard of play live

If we didn't expand our musical horizons, we'd still be chilling to 'Baa, Baa, Black Sheep' and other nursery rhymes. Despite reaching a decision some time ago that rare chamber music is your true groove, there's no need to shut off all other avenues for the rest of your life. After all, as Henry Ford once observed, 'Anyone who stops learning is old.'

Discovering a new artist whose music touches a nerve, makes you smile or cry, drives you to dance or soothes you to sleep, is one of the enduring joys of this life. Don't let anything stand in the way of that discovery. Be it a modern band or a hidden gem of a sixties' star, music is the gift that keeps on giving. So why not take the bull by the horns? Forget about timidly trying before you buy at the online record store – go straight to the frontline. Find out when there's a live act next booked at your local bar, then mosey on down to the mosh pit. Open your mind. The band might be crap; they also might be the Next Big Thing.

Stop the traffic

Once in your lifetime you should look so jaw-droppingly, drop-dead gorgeous that the traffic stops for you. After all, when you're old and grey and the only time anyone stops for you is if a Scout is helping you across the road, it will comfort you to look back at the time you almost caused a pile-up on the high street – for all the right reasons. Ways to achieve this could include:

- The tried-and-tested route of purchasing high heels and a long, blonde wig. There's just something about blonde hair, no matter about the front view. This works well if you're a woman – but you'll stop even more traffic if you're dressed like this and you're a man.
- Volunteering for a TV makeover programme. Not only will you get cut and pasted for free, but the very presence of a cameraman on your tail will make everyone stop and look at you.

If all else fails:

- Steal a traffic stop sign and bravely march towards

oncoming vehicles.
- Lie down in the middle of the road and pray.
- Strip.

Of course, you could just press the button at the pedestrian crossing, couldn't you?

Google yourself on the Internet

If you don't register on the first page of hits, act so as to ensure that you will next time you check.

Get creative

And you won't achieve it by crashing out on the sofa night after night. Remember all those short stories you used to write when you were small? Ever mime in front of the mirror or in your dad's garage in time to your favourite band? Well, what happened to all that inspiration and creativity? No matter – get it back, right here, right now, and show the world that there's more to you than IT consulting/shop assisting/land managing. Here's how:

- Write. Be it a short story, poem, play or novel, just express yourself. Not sure where to begin? Make it autobiographical. Take notes on funny conversations that you have with your friends and eavesdrop on people on the train. Steal people's gregarious personalities and trap them within the pages of your manuscript. Don't worry about the morals of doing this: it's all grist to the mill for the budding writer. Once satisfied with your masterpiece, get an agent, get a publishing deal, and become an overnight success.*

- Paint. Anything from the next *Mona Lisa* to your bedroom ticks the box. Choose colours that convey your emotions. (N.B. Don't decorate on a Monday morning with a hangover, or you'll be seducing Goths until you can afford to replace the black paint job.)
- Compose a song. Unfortunately, pressing the demo button on your electronic keyboard doesn't cut the mustard here – though it may impress a handful of people born before 1950. If you don't play an instrument, use your voice to create a hardcore rap/teenybopper pop medley/grunge chorus, according to taste.

---

* May be easier said than done.

Be thrown out of a bar

In all likelihood, you'll have managed this at least ten times during your college years alone. Being a lairy student, or just obviously underage with an unpersuasive fake ID, is unlikely to be relevant these days, however, so it's time to get a little bit more imaginative. Relish this final fling with irresponsibility, and care not a jot if it's your partner rather than your parents picking up the pieces when you roll in the door at 3 a.m.

Your first problem is that bouncers think older punters are more trustworthy than those hordes of youths intent on getting smashed on alcopops. So getting thrown out of a bar at your age demands some creativity. You could try:

- Stripping on the tables.*
- Having an affair with the bar manager and/or their partner: *respect* if you successfully engineer a soap-style showdown with accompanying recriminatory arguments.
- Wearing a hooded top. It's such a symbol of social anarchy that the bouncer will have you out on your ear before you've even had a chance to order that glass of fine red.
- If all else fails, drinking yourself into oblivion (perhaps as part of a *lost weekend*). You'll be thrown out of the joint eventually, either at the end of the night, or once you're lying in a pool of your own vomit (whichever comes first).

* Be warned, if you're any good, you could be booked for a regular slot, rather than being shown the door.

Get into a cab and shout, 'Follow that car!'

You've seen it in the movies, now make it part of your real life. Holler your instructions to the driver as you're getting into the cab. This way everyone in the street will hear and assume you're a government spy or a private detective. Wear a trench coat to enhance the effect. Avoid leaping into your chosen cab while the road is choked with traffic; twiddling your thumbs while stuck in a jam, your vehicular prey just one car ahead and within obvious walking distance, makes you look a fool. Instead, pick a fast-moving thoroughfare like a dual carriageway; your cabbie will be required to switch lanes with the capriciousness of a heartbreaker switching favourites. As you slide from side to side on the leather seat, always leaning slightly forwards to catch sight of that elusive motor, relish the feelings of drama, pace and excitement. Keep your fingers crossed that the car in front is not intent on a long journey. Keep your credit card on you just in case it is.

Keep a diary

Anne Frank did it, and went down in history. Jeffrey Archer did it, to a rather less reverential reception. But you, too, could follow in the footsteps of these illustrious diarists by recording the scandals of your life and times, together with the inevitable helpings of mundane minutiae.

Dig out your teenage diaries from the loft. Before cringing with embarrassment and burning them to ashes, stop a minute. Those memories are what make you who you are. So why not keep a new record of your 'mid youth', so you can wallow in nostalgia when you read them again at the age of eighty?

Record vice, debauchery, betrayal and passion with not a hint of coyness or of guilt. If your life contains none of the above, work your way through this book and that'll soon change.

Remember to note down the less obvious things, too. Seventeenth-century writer Samuel Pepys would describe his intake of cake and, oddly, asparagus, in amongst key events such as the Great Fire of London and the Plague, so follow his lead. One man's food diary is another's important historical document.

Spare no detail, however salacious. Twenty years from now, you'll re-read the saucy bits and think: 'Oh yes. I lived.'

Become someone's muse

Tell your boss where to shove their job

Now be honest: you can't say you've never thought about it. Be it bidding farewell to the Saturday job from your teenage years or quitting your twenty-year career, nothing beats the satisfaction of saying 'I'm outta here' to your incumbent employer. Maybe you've already thrown in the towel on a job or two ('I'll shoot myself if I have to clean another septic tank'), in which case, heartfelt congratulations! If you're currently stuck in a mind-numbingly boring job, however – those dreams of farming for a living nothing but a distant memory – what on earth is stopping you from reclaiming your life from the daily grind and making those ambitions a reality? Do it today. Hand in your notice, hand over your credit card to the nearest bartender, and drink the bar dry in celebration.

Of course, it helps if you have another job lined up, or a plan to travel the world – in fact, anything which sounds exciting and is likely to provoke both envy and awe in your employer and erstwhile colleagues. 'I've won the lottery', 'I've got a six-figure publishing deal', 'I've just been signed to Madonna's record label' or 'I'm starring in the next Steven Spielberg film' are good choices (and if you *get creative* or *audition for something*, some of those career paths may not actually be too far from the truth). At times, however, the simple yet effective 'I'd rather be *anywhere* else but here' parting shot can be just as gratifying to deliver.

TOP TIPS:

- If you're expecting a bonus, wait till it's safely in your bank account before staging your set-to with the boss.
- If you leave a massive workload/catalogue of errors behind you, you'll find that your departure seems even sweeter.
- Go for gardening leave for top-of-the-range revenge.

Learn to drive

Do you really want to get to forty without having passed your driving test? That's possibly half your life dependent on other drivers or, heaven forbid, public transport, to get you from A to B. Just think where you could go, at any time of the day or night, if you could drive your own car. (And just how much more shopping you could carry.) Unlimited freedom and independence could be yours – although it's fair to say you might get roped into ferrying others around, especially if you *have a baby*.

If you can already drive, take your motoring skills to the next level. Sample a circuit track, or go off-roading or on an extreme rallying course. Free from the hassles of speed cameras and plodding pedestrians, you can zoom with unlimited zest. Not only will your adrenalin go into overdrive as you tackle the drive of your life, but you'll also get the ultimate lesson in handbrake turns, oversteer, understeer and the racing line. The school run will never be quite the same again.

Experience a different religious service to your own

John F. Kennedy once said, 'If I had to live my life over again, I would have . . . a different religion.' Well, why wait until you're reincarnated? (If you're a Hindu or Buddhist, that is.) Experience a different religious service in your current lifetime. Not necessarily to change your religion, but rather to open your mind to different beliefs and practices, and to appreciate the aesthetics of another faith. Why not visit a different place of worship? Many buildings associated with religion are breathtakingly beautiful. Or read the Bible or the Koran, to understand better the ethos and history of the different creeds.

TOP TIPS:

- Attend a Catholic mass.
- Celebrate a Jewish bar mitzvah.
- Dance at an Indian wedding.
- Sing at a Christmas carol service.
- Join in Eid celebrations.
- Visit a mosque; a cathedral; a synagogue; a Buddhist, Sikh or Hindu temple; a Baptist, Methodist or Orthodox church.
- Answer the door to the Jehovah's Witnesses.

Learn a poem by heart

Swap houses

Sometimes, you just need a change of scenery to boost your spirits. So why not swap houses with someone? If you're canny, you can *find out how the other half lives* at the same time.

The Internet is awash with people looking for house swaps. Make your choice carefully. An illegal immigrant may be more than willing to open their home to you and yours, but a) a week in a war-torn city is not quite what you had in mind and b) will you ever get your own home back?

You could swap houses with someone abroad or with someone who lives in the same country as you do. You could do it for a week or a month. If you find yourself living in a celebrity's home, *sell your story to the tabloids*.

Cook a three-course meal from scratch

To get to your age you must have eaten a substantial number of substantial meals, so your culinary skills should be up to scratch, right? Interesting then, that many of us eat properly only in restaurants or at our mothers', or think the kitchen is a woman's place, or live on takeaways and posh pre-packaged nosh from M&S. Shame on you, go sharpen your kitchen knives.

Remember, cooking doesn't have to be complicated (leave that to the hired chef!). Most people would prefer to be served with a simple shepherd's pie than a dish overloaded with taste and texture. Stick to seasonal produce, prepare the starter and dessert well in advance of your guests' arrival, and you can't really go wrong.

You could even make an event of it. Soften the lights, crack open a bottle of fine wine, perhaps even hire a friend to act as a butler. Having basked in the praise of your satiated guests, you can relax with the box of luxury chocolates. Pass the port, will you?

Read a Russian novel

They say that nothing that can be done too easily is worth doing. So pluck up some stamina and wade into the Russian novel – epic entertainment at its best. Recommended reads are as follows:

- *Eugene Onegin* by Aleksandr Pushkin (a novel written in verse).
- *A Hero of Our Time* by Mikhail Lermontov.
- *Dead Souls* by Nikolai Gogol.
- *Crime and Punishment* by Fyodor Dostoevsky.
- *War and Peace* and *Anna Karenina* by Count Leo Tolstoy.
- *Fathers and Sons* by Ivan Turgenev.

See a foreign film

Talking of getting cultured, why not branch out a little in your choice of home movie? There are loads to choose from. Perhaps you could consider some of the following?

- *The Seven Samurai*, directed by Akira Kurosawa.
- *The Seventh Seal*, directed by Ingmar Bergman.
- *Bicycle Thieves*, directed by Vittorio De Sica.
- *Amélie*, directed by Jean-Pierre Jeunet.
- *The 400 Blows*, directed by François Truffaut.
- *La Dolce Vita*, directed by Federico Fellini.
- *Raise the Red Lantern*, directed by Yimou Zhang.
- *Breathless*, directed by Jean-Luc Godard.
- *Cinema Paradiso*, directed by Giuseppe Tornatore.
- *Das Boot*, directed by Wolfgang Petersen.
- *Au Revoir, les Enfants*, directed by Louis Malle.
- *Crouching Tiger, Hidden Dragon*, directed by Ang Lee.
- *Jean de Florette*, directed by Claude Berri.
- *Life is Beautiful*, directed by Roberto Benigni.

Get married in Vegas (for 48 hours)

If it's good enough for Britney, it's good enough for you. You'll note there's an optional time limit on this challenge (though if you end up married to a damn fine stripper, you may wish to rethink that particular element). This isn't 'till death us do part', it's only 'till all this alcohol wears off'. Like any wedding, there are certain essentials you cannot do without (a bride and groom being key), but the actual planning should really take no longer than the time it takes to say, 'Fancy getting hitched?'

TOP TIPS:

- Book a comedy priest.
- Wear outlandish outfits.
- Have an Elvis impersonator as a witness.
- Choose the tackiest venue you've ever seen.
- Get an upgrade to the honeymoon suite at your hotel.
- Sign the divorce papers.

Become a swinger

Don't leave it till your swinging sixties to have some fun on the side. If you think your relationship could include less routine and more recreation, why not get together for a good romp with some like-minded people? The more the merrier, if that's the way you like it. Remember, swinging isn't just about having sex – it's about exploring your sexuality and the meaning of love, and about learning to express yourself and being honest about your needs and desires. Swingers believe that sex is as natural as eating and drinking, and that sharing our bodies is not at all shameful.

Admittedly, this isn't going to be everyone's cup of tea. But there's another sort of swinger you can be and still have fun . . . the kind that can never resist the swing in the park or playground. Go for it! The kids will stare at you, but you're only a big kid yourself.

Change the way you look

Okay, so clearly you look different now from when you first came into the world, screaming your head off and stark bollock naked. Time waits for no man, no matter how much Elizabeth Arden Eight-hour Cream he applies. But with age comes freedom: the freedom to put your own mark on your appearance. Seize the day and banish image insecurities for good. If you're not impressed with what God gave you, simple. Change it. Your mum might have said no to facial piercings when you were young, but what's stopping you now? You could:

- Get a tattoo (or get rid of one – 'I Love Sheep' doesn't always translate from one culture to the next).
- Get yourself pierced (whichever adornment floats your boat – from ear lobes and noses to tongues and trousersnakes).
- Dye your hair – or shave your head.
- Have plastic surgery: an extreme, but ever more popular choice, thanks to the likes of Pamela Anderson and other, sometimes more coy, celebrities (but definitely not Michael Jackson).

- Get a wardrobe makeover. Out with the geeky garments, in with the chic professional look.
- Lose or gain shedloads of weight. Shock yourself with a brand-new shape.

Blag your way backstage

Date someone unsuitable

Why? Well, it's fun. Mischievous. All your friends will disapprove (and be slightly jealous). The relationship will have that edge of danger, an element of impishness, the spice of forbidden fruit. So it's not going to end in marriage and babies. Who cares? In fact, that's the whole point. Have a wild affair with someone completely inappropriate. If you've already ticked this particular box, you'll know that spirited abandon with which one approaches this kind of liaison. It's a rollercoaster ride of daredevil dates and lost inhibitions. Just be prepared for the *messy break-up* when it all comes crashing down around your ears.

TOP TIPS:

- Seduce someone significantly younger — or older — than you are.
- Step out with a celebrity.
- Court a colleague (even your boss!).
- Steal someone else's squeeze.

Buy a house

Along with *learning to drive*, *having a baby* and *learning how to programme the video recorder*, buying a house is one of those rites of passage that you really need to go through if you want to call yourself a grown-up. In fact, there's no surer way of announcing your adulthood than becoming a fully paid-up member of the property-owning classes. Of course, if you haven't done it already, you'll have no shortage of smug friends delighting in pointing out how much money they've made on the property ladder and how you really should have got on the first rungs twenty years ago. But it's not too late. With a little dedication and hard work, you too can be the proud owner of the stately pile in the country, the romantic log cabin, the modernist studio shag pad or – more likely – the cosy little two-up-two-down in the suburbs. Whatever, it'll be home. To decorate as your own personal whims and fancies take you.

You'll need your wits about you as you negotiate the minefield of estate agents, mortgage brokers, solicitors, vendors and endless chains, but you will come out the other side a poorer (much poorer) yet happy homeowner. And you'll have enough hard-won knowledge of the outrageous state of the property market to keep you in dinner-party conversations (staged in your lovely new open-plan kitchen/diner, natch) for years.

Visit hot springs

Ah, the stomach-churning smell of sulphur, the plop and splash of bubbling mud, and the occasional electrifying whoosh of a geyser in full spurt – yes, everyone should enjoy the unique experience of a genuine hot springs while they're still nimble enough to dodge the deadly bursts of steam. If the springs are attached to a luxury spa, where you can take the restorative waters and get a full-body massage as part of the package, so much the better.

Do:
Mind your step and stick to the paths – if you're in an

area of volcanic activity, you sure as hell don't want to step back on to a live geyser while you're positioning yourself for the best photograph.

Don't:
Breathe in through your nose.

Good places to see hot springs:

- Yellowstone National Park, Wyoming, USA – home of the postcard-friendly Old Faithful geyser, but did you know it contains around 500 others too, which is half the world's total number?
- North Island, New Zealand.
- Iceland – home of the famous Blue Lagoon.
- El Tatio, Chile.

Forgive someone

That bloke who trod on your toe as he pushed past you to get on the train this morning? That teacher who told you, aged twelve, that you would never amount to anything? The lover who broke your heart so badly that the scar still aches?

Take a deep breath. Smile benignly. Forgive. By the age of forty it's high time you learned one of life's greatest secrets – that if someone hurts you and you forgive them, it's *you* who will feel better for it.

Learn a new word every day for a month

Express yourself through the medium of dance

'Done that!' you may scoff. Ah, but have you? Admittedly, if you're a member of the English National Ballet or Wayne Sleep, you probably have, but the rest of you: take note. This isn't just about boogying to Blondie or shaking your stuff at the school disco all those years ago. This is about letting go: forgetting the room, yourself and especially the fancy footwork. Next time you're out on the town or getting down in the privacy of your own living room, let that demon dancing queen or king inside of you take control. Dance like no one's watching. Savour the sensuality of your own body as you move to the music. Fling out limbs with the new-found freedom of one recently released from a straitjacket. Headbang like a hedonist. Feels good, doesn't it? If truly inspired, make up your own dance routines that will wow strangers and shame relatives in equal measure.

Have Tea at the Ritz

Once the preserve of society ladies and gentlemen, Tea at the Ritz is now accessible to all and sundry (so long as men wear a jacket and tie and we all abstain from donning jeans and trainers). You'll have to book six weeks in advance, but the opportunity to soak up a century of sophistication is well worth the wait. Within those hallowed walls, Sir Winston Churchill and President Eisenhower met for clandestine war meetings; Noël Coward composed on the baby grand; Tallulah Bankhead sipped champagne from her slipper; and you stuffed yourself with miniature pastries to your heart's content. Ah, we all have our talents. If you've already done the Ritz, darling, make it your mission in life to have afternoon tea at every five-star hotel in London. And please, let's all remember to extend that pinkie when we do take tea: it wouldn't be the same without it.

Track down your first love

There's nothing like first love. It can affect the way you feel about relationships for ever, and all other lovers will be compared to that first – good or bad.

It's actually quite a cathartic experience to track down the person who first stole your heart. For example, if you have romanticized them, how would you feel about them if you saw them with frown lines instead of freckles? Perhaps, after all this time, you could make a friend of them? Or, if they broke your heart, you could make peace with them – after all, perhaps it's now time to *forgive someone* as you approach middle age.

Of course, if you married your first love you won't have to look too far, will you – except perhaps for the love you started out with. But let's not be cynical – love can last a lifetime!

TOP TIPS:

- Check the phone book.
- Ask long-time friends for leads.
- Look up your old lover on Friends Reunited.
- *Visit your old school.*
- Google them.
- Hire a private detective.
- *Send a message in a bottle.*

Visit the wonders of the world

Well, there were seven – once. Sadly most of these succumbed to earthquake, wind and fire, and the like, though the Great Pyramid of Giza stands strong to this day. Still, the world is full of wonders and you want to make sure that you have ticked all its boxes. It's just that now there are rather a lot of them. Feel free to make a start here.

Before I am forty, I must see . . .

- Abu Simbel Temples, Egypt.
- Angkor Wat, Cambodia.
- The Colosseum, Rome.
- The Eiffel Tower, Paris.

- The Empire State Building, New York.
- The Golden Gate Bridge, San Francisco.
- The Grand Canyon, Arizona.
- The Great Barrier Reef, Australia.
- The Great Wall of China.
- The Hoover Dam, Arizona.
- The Leaning Tower of Pisa, Italy.
- Machu Picchu, Peru.
- Mount Everest, Nepal.
- Mount Rushmore National Memorial, South Dakota.
- Niagara Falls, Ontario (Canada) and New York State (USA).
- The Panama Canal, Panama.
- The Parthenon, Athens.
- The Statue of Cristo Redentor, Rio de Janeiro.
- The Statue of Liberty, New York.
- Stonehenge, England.
- The Suez Canal, Egypt.
- The Sydney Opera House, Australia.
- Victoria Falls, Zambia/Zimbabwe.

Streak at a major sporting event

Want to be a sporting legend, but lack the talent? Well, there's another way to get into the hall of fame. Why not just take your clothes off and run for it?

The advantages:

- You get to have your picture taken by hundreds of people.
- You get in the papers.
- You might earn a few pounds by *selling your story to the tabloids*.

The disadvantages:

- You get chased and caught and arrested by the police.
- You might have to *spend the night in police cells*.

If the thought of stripping off sends shivers down your spine (and for all the wrong reasons), think about simply attending a major sporting event, instead. Ever seen an England World Cup match (football or rugby)? Watched the rain at Wimbledon? Taken in athletics track-and-field events? Next time there's a Championship coming up – in any sport – get yourself to the heart of the action as a spectator. Not only will you get to see your sporting idols play live, you'll have front-row seats when all those foolhardy, not-quite-forty-somethings start streaking . . .

Give a stranger in the street a bunch of flowers

As they say, Say It With Flowers. Say what, exactly?

- I thought you looked a little down. Would these make you smile?
- Excuse me, I couldn't help noticing these cornflowers are the exact shade of your eyes.
- You're doing such a good job sweeping the street/ directing the traffic that I thought you deserved a reward.
- She doesn't love me, please take these (and can I have your phone number?).
- I'm going to make you feel happy.
- I'm going to make you feel really awkward.
- I fancy you.
- Giving is better than receiving.

Why before you're forty? Flowers from an octogenarian aren't quite the same, are they?

Make at least one friend for life

They were there with you on your first day at primary school; when you fell off your bike and broke your arm; when your dog died; when you won the 100 metres; when you went to your first club; the day you passed your test and drove your own car; and when you went on your first holiday without mum and dad. Now, even though you are both out there in the big wide world, you are still 100 per cent there for each other – whenever the going's good, and whenever the chips are down. No fair-weathered friend here. You'll be each other's bridesmaid or best man, and godparents to each other's children. On your fortieth birthdays, you'll not only be there to wish each other well and to drink the bubbly, but you'll know you've got a friend for life.

Ride an animal

Whether or not Black Beauty was your childhood idol, by the time you reach forty you should have ridden an animal. And not just for the practicality of getting from A to B or for the thrill of dressing up in skintight jodhpurs (though see *make a fashion faux pas* and *act out a sexual fantasy*, in case you're considering the latter). Riding an animal is one of the quirkiest, most unusual experiences you can have in life. Feeling the flesh of another living creature beneath you, the strength in their limbs, the vitality in their movements, is something that cannot be recreated any other way. Just be warned that they're not quite as biddable as taxi drivers. If horses leave you feeling cold, why not try an elephant instead? The world's largest land mammals are majestic creatures, so you're bound to be King of the Road astride one. Or how about a camel, a creature first domesticated 5,000 years ago; or the humble donkey, famed for carrying Mary all the way to Bethlehem? If it's good enough for the Mother of God . . .

Have a messy break-up

The tears, the accusations, the complicated death throes of that lingering attraction: ah, the joys of the messy break-up. We've all been there: broken someone's heart and then gone back for more just as they were getting over us (there's nothing like sleeping with the ex for great, great sex). And we've been on the receiving end of such dastardly behaviour, too. The messy break-up is something that just has to be experienced. How else would we appreciate all those mournful love songs? Singledom never tastes so sweet as when we've walked over broken glass to get there, extricating ourselves in the most painful way possible from a relationship long since dead, but kept alive through the black arts and mere routine. To appreciate the grand masters of the messy break-up, *read a Russian novel*. They really have it down to a fine art – revenge, ruin, suicide, murder . . . it makes a little bit of property damage and the odd nervous breakdown look like child's play in comparison.

Change your eating habits
for a month

It's all too easy to get stuck in a food rut. One moment you'll try all manner of delicacies on your palette, including self-made mud pies; the next, you've the blinkered attitude of Andy from *Little Britain*: 'I want that one,' and that one alone. Why not shake things up a bit? Change your eating habits for one month and see where it leaves you. If you eat meat, go veggie: see if the grass is greener when all you eat are greens. If veggie, try the more extreme vegan diet. Attempt a detox for a month – your body will thank you for it, possibly with increased flatulence, but more likely with weight loss and shiny hair. Experiment with new recipes and novel foodstuffs. Eat the things you've only read about in books. If you normally stick to the fare of one country – perhaps Italy, with mounds of pasta and oven-baked pizzas – travel a little instead. Consume the cuisine of Calcutta, or the fodder of the French. After all, if you watched the same film over and over again, you'd soon get bored of it. The same goes for your diet. So don't be dull – dare to dine differently.

Buy a sex toy

Never bought yourself a sex toy? Well, you should, because they're fun – and even high-street shops sell them these days. Now there are sex toys and sex toys, and we're not talking chocolate willies and pink fluffy handcuffs. Girls, if you've never bought a Rabbit then do so today. Not the fluffy sort that lives in a cage, you understand. (Quite a few women don't understand this, which can be embarrassing for them if the conversation is about the other sort.) To be clear on this, we mean the type that means you'll never have to worry about having an orgasm again. And guys, if you really want to please the lady in your life, forget buying her the nurse outfit – just buy the Rabbit. No need to feel threatened; she still loves you more – well, out of bed anyway. At any rate, you can't cuddle a vibrator.

Learn how to programme
the video recorder

This is possibly more directed at the girls out there. Having a husband is no excuse for not being able to work the video recorder, although you could argue it is fair exchange for him not being able to work the washing machine. Or a good excuse for not being able to tape the footie. ('I don't know how it recorded *Desperate Housewives*, honest.')

So, if you are under forty and have no obvious disabilities (other than not being able to work a simple machine), you should be more than capable of getting down on your knees to press the button with the word 'record' on it. (Sadly the remote control seems to be a 'man thing' too.) Just dig out the manual and work your way through it – you'll feel like you've cracked Fermat's Last Theorem when you've achieved it. If you're really hopeless, do not attempt the higher levels of 'timer record'. Just be prepared to rewind for hours before you get to the programme you actually wanted to watch.

Finally, the fact that DVDs are taking over from video is not a way out here. We're talking principles – and anyhow, you'll just have to learn to record on the DVD machine.

Research and write up your family tree

Handle a tarantula

. . . But only if you're scared of spiders. Yes, the time has come to face your greatest fears – and overcome them. You cannot pass the forty-year milestone without at least attempting to do battle with the metaphorical monster in your closet, so take a deep breath, enlist the help of a very good friend or therapist, and strike a path towards a life without fear, without shame, without the night sweats. You know you can do it. We'll, um, see you on the other side.

- Walk through a field with a bull in it.
- Go caving and turn off your headlamp for a full two minutes.
- Stroke an Alsatian. Pet his pit bull friend. Hold your nerve while they bark louder than the drum solo at a heavy-metal concert.

- Sing 'I'm leaving on a jet plane' . . . and then actually fly somewhere.
- Cast aside your fears of commitment and tie the knot. What's the worst that could happen?
- Catch a cable car up a bona fide mountain. Take in the view. Look down. Look down again. Hold the gaze of that motherf**king scary chasm below. If you're feeling really brave, abseil or bungee jump into it.

Pretend you are a sexy foreigner

Woo members of the opposite sex with
your fake accent.

Take an evening class

Do you sometimes wish you'd paid more attention in the classroom? So why not go back there? Okay, you've probably been out of education for a long time now, but that's no excuse; and neither is that you work or look after the kids all day. They run schools at night for people like you.

You could start by learning a language – French or Spanish for the holiday, Chinese for the CV. Or how about learning to tell the difference between Pinot and plonk? Flower arranging, anyone?

Reasons why you should take an evening class:

- No one should rest on their laurels.
- The school of life does not teach you everything you should have learned at school.

- It builds self-confidence.
- It will get you out of the home and take your mind off the kids, partner, job – or, for that matter, your lack of kids, partner, job.
- You'll make new friends.
- You can talk about something new.
- You'll dedicate time to improving yourself – rather than your children's homework or your boss's bonus.
- Acquiring a new skill or qualification can lead to a Better, Brighter Future (the slogan of many an adult-education scheme).

Find out how the other half lives

Throw caution to the wind and sample all the deluxe delights that twenty-first-century life has to offer. Like Craig David, you may find that you were born to do it. Why not:

- Travel in style. Hire a Mercedes/Ferrari/helicopter/limousine for the day, and really make an entrance.
- Drink vintage wine and champagne. Order the most expensive bottle of wine in a restaurant – without blinking or sweating profusely. Be cool.
- Indulge in a money-is-no-object weekend away – first-class travel, top-class restaurants, book the penthouse suite in the best hotel in town. If you're feeling really daring, go mad and drink something from the mini-bar – it may well cost more than the room itself.
- Spend a day at the races. Hats are essential, bullish gambling is de rigueur, the cut-glass, upper-class accent is an optional extra. Make sure you spend any winnings on something frivolous like a racehorse or a villa in Monte Carlo.

Have sex in public

Maybe you've done it on the boss's desk, or in a car; maybe you can even claim to be a member of the Mile High Club. But have you ever had sex in a really public place? So what if people can see what you are up to? That's the fun of it!

So how about sex in a lift? In a phone booth? Or how about a photo booth? (You could photograph yourself in the act.) If you're really daring, you could have sex on a train – although your typical rail passenger will probably hide behind a newspaper and pretend nothing's happening.

You could inject a little romance. How about sex in a rowing boat? Or sex on the beach? (Better in Barbados, admittedly, but Brighton will do.) Or why not the balcony of a hotel? The swimming pool?

If you like to stay close to home, experiment on the patio. There's always the local park or beauty spot, too. If you're a novice at this, don't dismiss the quickie in a dark alleyway or doorway. Whatever you do, just don't get to forty thinking the only place to have sex is under the bedclothes.

Be a mentor to someone younger than you

In your youth, your attitude to colleagues might simply have been to see their heads as convenient stepping stones to scramble over as you hauled your way to the top of the corporate tree. But with age comes a realization that it doesn't have to be this way. If you are

fortunate enough to have risen to the top, ask yourself how you want to be seen now that you've made the transition from hungry young buck to elder states(wo)man. Do you want to be the approachable, generous, wise old boss whose door is always open? Or the hard-faced, insecure workaholic, always looking over their shoulder at the young guns coming up behind in the fast lane? Let's face it, it won't be long before those fresh-faced pixies are running the show. Don't fight it – instead enjoy that feeling of nurturing and teaching the little chicks and watching them protectively as they fly the nest.

Still need convincing? Remember: that skinny guy weighed down by reference books, diligently checking facts, or that bright-eyed girl working late every night, trying to figure out the best way to put together the presentation – they were you, twenty years ago. Do them a favour, and extend a helping hand.

Have a full medical check-up

Drive a tractor

We all know what it feels like to be stuck behind a tractor on a country road. Just your luck, he's heading for the farm a mile or more further on, and he isn't intending to pull over before then – especially not for you. But before you get all stressed out, pause for a minute. For starters, remember that speeding along country lanes is a hazardous activity that may result in a head-on with a tractor approaching from the other direction. You do want to get to forty, don't you?

So if you can't overtake them, why not join them? Have you ever considered what it feels like to be the guy driving the tractor – the king of the country road, chugging through life, cheerfully ignoring the twelve-car traffic jam on his tail?

Jokes about 'can't read, can't write, but can drive a tractor' apart, tractor driving is the new motorized sport. And if you think it looks easy, wait till you try tractor-and-trailer slaloming, where not only do you have to drive the beast between poles, but reverse it backwards through the course. It's a whole new challenge and you'll never look at a tractor in the same way again.

Smoke a pipe

If packing your bags seems a bit old hat, why not learn to pack a pipe instead? Smoking a pipe will afford you regular periods of calm contemplation, which will relax you as much as any holiday, plus you get to join the ranks of such distinguished pipe smokers as Albert Einstein, Harold Wilson, John Coltrane, Bing Crosby, Vincent van Gogh, Virginia Woolf, Sherlock Holmes and, er, Popeye.

Now, no one says you are going to be Pipe Smoker of the Year in one puff (please don't inhale, by the way). However, if you are going to get serious about it, you will be introduced to a whole new world of pipes and pipe accessories, to say nothing of a myriad tobacco types.

So the next time someone mentions Virginia, Kentucky, Latakia, Turkish or Oriental, don't think plane tickets, think tobacco. Gordon Bennett! (Yes, you can put that in your pipe and smoke it, too.)

Sell your story to the tabloids

Forget about the ethics: think about the fame (or infamy). Everyone deserves their fifteen minutes. For the best deals, hire a high-profile publicist. They'll ensure that your story reaches the masses for the common good. You'll later find that their invoice is directly in proportion to the size of your new-found wealth.

Going about it – top-selling stories:

- The kiss-and-tell. A timeless classic. Choose a good-looking victim to enhance your physical enjoyment of the affair; choose a rich one to ensure great gifts. Select the fetish-loving exhibitionist for an exquisitely expensive Sunday-paper scoop. For even more fruitful financial rewards, rope in the brother/business partner/wife/mother (or all four) for a real money-making ménage.
- Win something. Obviously, the more high profile it is, the better. 'Employee of the month' might not quite have the nationals storming down your door, but you may get an interview with the trade press.
- Dress up as a fake sheik.

Become a street performer

Ever looked at those 'living statues' clogging up the pavements near tourist traps and thought to yourself, 'What a ridiculous way to make a buck'? Ever tutted disapprovingly as you pushed past the crowd gathering round an inept juggler wobbling about on a unicycle? Or sneered at the guy playing the penny whistle outside the supermarket? Well, shame on you. It takes guts to stand up in front of a group of strangers and throw yourself on their mercy. In fact, it's an essential rite of passage. Do it once, just for the rush. Release your inner Marcel Marceau! Then quickly mime stuffing him back into his transparent box before you get too carried away.

Stand up for what you believe in

You can't spend your whole life sitting on the fence, refusing to be drawn on your opinions. Stand up and be counted. Make your views known. Make a difference. Be it your political perspective, a friendship or even a decision at work, be firm about what you think and defend your position to the hilt. Find your own voice and speak out.

TOP TIPS:

- Go on a demo or march.
- Vote in an election.
- Write to your MP.
- Start a campaign, perhaps as *part of your local community*.
- Have a political discussion.
- Defend someone.

Visit your old school

It's odd how nervous you can be about going back to your old school. It's the feeling you get when you stay with your parents for more than a weekend – no matter how successful and independent you are, you are suddenly waiting to be ticked off for having untidy hair or for not having done your homework.

Of course, some of us loved school, but even if you eagerly anticipate that annual newsletter, you may not have actually been back to the place or seen your fellow pupils for a long time.

So, should we call the whole thing off? Correct answer: no. It's good to reflect on where we've come from, and who and what made us who we are today. If you want support, why not get an old school friend to come too? Or organize a full-on class reunion? (Purportedly to renew old friendships and celebrate your mutual successes; in reality the chance to suss out who you've bettered, and whether the cute classmate is now fat.) It's amazing how chuffed you'll feel after you realize the school swot never did do much with those straight As.

Smash something out of sheer frustration – the bigger the better!

It's an odd fact that breaking something brings with it an immense feeling of calm and relief – providing you don't care too much about the object in question, or any persons caught in the line of fire.

Good things to smash:

- Your partner's car (you can still drive yours, after all).
- A wine collection.
- Your parents' Lladro or other china ornaments.
- Freebie coffee mugs.
- Your child's Gameboy.
- Someone else's mobile phone.
- An ice cream into someone's face.

Bad things to smash:

- Any person or animal.
- The telly (now how are you going to watch your favourite soap or the footie?).
- Photographs (it's not worth losing your happy memories in a moment's unhappiness).
- Wedding gifts (you might get back together . . . the crystal and china won't).
- Your own mobile phone.
- The house (far too much mess to clean up afterwards).

Public Safety Warning: It is dangerous to throw computers, TVs, sofas, yourself or other people out of windows.

Tell your mother you love her

If there's one person to whom you owe a great, great deal in this life, it's your mother. Not only for the whole carrying-you-for-nine-months thing (though fair dues to her there, the girl done good), but for all the other small, huge, wonderful contributions she's made, to make you the person you are today. Doesn't she deserve a little payback? She, of course, would answer no – because that's what mothers are like: selfless, a little self-deprecating, doing it all because they love you unconditionally. But, hey, you know what? You love her unconditionally too. So show her. Better yet, tell her.

Embrace her in a massive bear hug, hold her tight, and say the words: 'I love you.'

If your relationship with your mother isn't great, isn't it about time to bury the hatchet? (No, not in her head.) Nearly forty years is a long time to hold a grudge. Maybe take this as your opportunity to *forgive someone*.

One of the worst things about getting older is that your parents get older, too. They're not going to be around for ever, more's the pity. So appreciate them 100 per cent today. Make sure they know you're truly grateful for all they did (grounding you when you were seventeen and had an invite to the party-to-end-all-parties notwithstanding). For all the years that your mother was there for you, be there for her too. Be thankful. Above all, make those three little words the most important ones she'll ever hear from you, because they are the ones that matter most.

Eat an unusual dish from another culture

Is eating a German sausage the 'wurst' thing you could imagine? Or do the following whet your appetite?

- Crocodile steaks, ostrich burgers and smoked emu (lunch Down Under, anyone?).
- Elephant or zebra steaks (book your ticket to Kenya).
- Guinea pig and chips (South American dish).
- Piranha salad (if you fancy a nibble, it's off to Brazil).
- Sea slug with cashews (when dining in Vietnam).
- Seaweed or fugu* (as eaten in Japan).
- Dog for dinner (if you're barking, try it in China).
- Frogs' legs or snails (a delicacy or cliché when *en France*).
- Deep-fried grasshoppers (one night when in Bangkok).
- Ant eggs (don't make hard work of them in Thailand).**

See how much better the sausage sounds now?

*Health warning: the ovaries and liver of some puffer fish contain a powerful poison called tetrodotoxin. So be careful when partaking of this gourmet delicacy.

**There are nearly 1,500 recorded species of edible insects, so don't stop at ants.

Give up technology

We've all felt that rising panic when we realize we've left our mobile phone at home. We've all contemplated dashing back to get it, sure that we can't survive even a day without it. But of course, we can. We've all lived a time before mobiles, after all. So next time, don't dash back; walk calmly on and surrender yourself to a world without polyphonic ringtones and multimedia messages demanding your attention every second of the day. See how it feels. Once that initial dismay has subsided, there'll be peace and quiet. Freedom. No claims on you. Hell, switch off the Blackberry, too. Don't check your email for a week. If you're feeling really plucky, go a month without TV. Will you die if you don't catch the next episode of *Lost*? Give up technology. Actually see your friends in person instead. Read books. ***Plant a tree***. The world will seem a calmer place. Live your life at a slower pace. Chill out. Relinquish your command of txt spk and reacquaint yourself with proper English instead. Enjoy not being available 24/7. Give your thumbs a well-earned break.

Have an evening out by yourself

Forget about pyjamas in front of the telly, go on a real date – with yourself. Somewhere you really want to go . . . although remember you're paying.

Wherever you go, hold your head up high and show the world you are not embarrassed to eat at a table for one, to sit by yourself in the cinema, or embrace the dance floor alone. While you are bound to be self-conscious at first, don't show it. Do not tolerate or become flustered by rude waiters; refuse to change your table or your seat to accommodate larger parties; give creeps the brush off; and smile warmly at those who send you nosy or pitying glances.

During your date, ask yourself, 'Am I enjoying myself? Do I like to be and to be seen with me?' The answer you're aiming for is 'yes'.

Audition for something

Whether you're the kind of person who gets stage fright just by stepping into a theatre, or you're an exhibitionist luvvie born to perform, before you turn forty make sure you've auditioned for something. Whether or not you get cast, at least you'll have put yourself out there.

It takes a lot of guts to audition. Most people take deep breaths, square their shoulders and go for it. The Japanese film *Ôdishon* (*Audition*) has solutions of a different sort. If you **watch this foreign film**, be warned that it explores raw nerves in a rather more visceral way than you might be expecting.

If treading the boards fills you with trepidation, why not showcase some other skills instead?

- Audition to be a contestant on a game show.
- Secure a walk-on part in a film.
- Sing to Simon Cowell on a TV talent show.
- Join a band.

You never know, you could be harbouring hidden talents.

Look at the night sky through a telescope

There's nothing quite as mysterious or as bewitching as the night sky. An enigmatic expanse, billions of years old, that dwarfs and outlasts us all. Tip your head back and take it in. Isn't it spectacular?

Any astronomer will tell you that the naked eye reveals next to nothing, however. So take in the view through a telescope. Suddenly, everywhere you look there are stars (and we're not talking the Hollywood Walk of Fame). Remember that the night sky is a feast made more delicious for those who know what they are looking at. So you can pick out the Plough, but can you identify the Pleiades? Swot up on your stars and planets, or get help from someone who can point your telescope in the right direction.

TOP TIPS:

- Make sure the telescope is clean. You're not supposed to be looking at dust clouds on the lens.
- Head to the country to gaze at the heavens. The lack of light pollution will enhance your experience. You could *go camping*, and sleep under the same stars you're studying.
- The celestial bodies you can see will vary around the world. *Travel to every continent* and look at the night sky in each country you visit. What's the spectacle like when you're *standing on the Equator*?
- Don't pick a cloudy night.

Attempt an unusual sexual position

Whether you're decades into a long-term relationship or still showing nubile singletons the true meaning of free love every other weekend, your sex life should by now reflect your many years of experience on this journey we call Life.

But if your repertoire doesn't yet extend beyond the rote of him-on-top, her-on-top and from-behind-on-bonk-holidays, ask yourself why. While age does not bring with it the suppleness of youth, it should release your long-held – but wholly questionable – inhibitions. After all, if not now, then when? Swallow your pride (among other things), grab a copy of the *Kama Sutra*, and prepare to do battle with gravity, furniture and the flexibility of your own limbs. It will be worth it – nothing gives a bigger ego boost than pulling off (so to speak) an impossible pose, while some positions will truly blow the mind . . . and more.

Go camping

It's a fact of life that as you get older your taste for luxury increases. By forty you'll have lost the ability to holiday anywhere other than a five-star hotel. You need to get back to the simpler things in life. While you can still face it, why not start by sleeping in a tent?

In fact, camping has never been easier. No more banging in wooden pegs with a mallet, holding on to the tent flaps in a raging gale, or shivering in damp sleeping bags. Modern technology has provided us with tents more akin to homes than, well, tents. Today's canvas palaces come equipped with zippable front doors, kitchens, lounging areas and separate bedrooms. Showers? Well, come on, we are camping.

Of course, the romance of camping is not to be found at the campsite, but in peace and isolation under the stars. Light a fire; have a singsong; eat baked beans out of the saucepan; toast marshmallows on a stick; scare yourself witless with ghost stories; have a midnight feast; and prepare yourself for a near heart attack when a cow stumbles into the field at three in the morning.

Fire a gun

Not that we're advocating a gun culture, of course. But haven't you ever wondered what it would feel like? The cool touch of the metal against your skin, the power in the trigger, the unexpectedness of the recoil, the satisfaction of nailing your shot. There are a few, serious points to take into consideration though:

- Fire the gun in a controlled environment, i.e. in a shooting range or game preserve, rather than in a situation in which you have all the control (such as, a bank heist, or when chairing a board meeting).
- In the UK, it's illegal to own a handgun, and if you purchase any other kind of firearm, it must be licensed by the proper authorities. If you like firing a gun so much that you want to buy your own, make sure you check out the gun laws in full.
- When firing your gun, take full advantage of the rare opportunity to present your best Bruce Willis/Jodie Foster impression. You may never get another chance to do so.
- Don't kill or injure anyone.

Travel to every continent

When you're old and incontinent, wouldn't it be something to say that you'd set foot on each of the world's great land masses? So what are you waiting for?

Well, according to statistics, only 15 per cent of British people actually know what the continents are. Just in case you fall within that group (get ye to night school to *take an evening class* in geography!), they are Europe, Asia, Africa, Australasia, North America, South America and Antarctica.

That's seven of them if you're counting, and it doesn't matter in which order you visit, or how you get there – by sea, by air, by land, or by 'Beam me up, Scotty'.

Make it a round trip if you like, or seven separate holidays if that's your preference. Just get with the drift!

Make good on a drunken bet

The best ideas come to us when we've had a drink or two. Fired up not only by alcohol but by inspiration, a love of life and all it has to offer coursing through our veins, we challenge each other to seize the day, along with the world's wildest opportunities. In the cold light of morning, however, hangover throbbing at our temples and bile rising in our throats, we forget the pledges of the past few hours. It's cowardly, and it's foolish. Drunken dares invite us to live the dreams we give up on when we're sober. For just once in your life, let that fire burn for more than a drinking session, and make good on a drunken bet. Whether you then find

 yourself driving to Outer Mongolia in a clapped-out car, *starting your own business*, or hitchhiking round Ireland with a fridge (Tony Hawks not only made good on his bet, he also made a packet by writing it up into a bestselling book), you'll be living life to the full.

TOP TIPS:

- Leave a voicemail for yourself with details of your agreed mission.
- Scribble the blueprint of the bet on a couple of beer mats.
- Have the guts to remember the dare in the morning. Most of us recall what we do when we're drunk, but unlike inebriated tumbles and poor pulls, this could be something worth remembering.

Bury a time capsule

Have a baby

You will need:

- One egg.
- One sperm.
- At least one love-making session or an appointment with a turkey baster/test tube.
- A lot of courage, time, money and energy.

It's one of those things that seems like a good idea at the time. Later, after countless tantrums, unbelievably selfish acts and no recognition whatsoever for all you do (and that's just your evolving relationship with your partner, by the way), you sometimes want to rethink the whole thing. But there is nothing more incredible than making a new life. Those of you already with children will know that the rewards far cancel out the tribulations (though of course it's a close-run thing for the first six months). Those without: now might be the time to stop putting it off until some hazy future point. Whether or not your biological clock is ticking louder than Captain Hook's nemesis, we none of us are Peter Pan. Unless you fancy spending your pension on university fees, it's high time to cast out contraception and get down to the baby-making business.

Perhaps you're still not quite ready for such a commitment, however? Rewarding alternatives would be to get a pet or to babysit for friends' children (being able to hand back said kids at the end of the day will increase your patience with them tenfold). If even these suggestions are enough to bring you out in a cold sweat, though, take things even slower: managing to walk round Toys "R" Us without palpitations will be quite enough achievement for one day.

Gatecrash a wedding

Some of us just love a wedding. Trouble is, as you approach forty the wedding invitations on your mantelpiece will be dwindling, owing to a lack of unhitched friends. So unless your mates are on to second marriages, it's a long wait until their children walk down the aisle. What the heck, go gatecrash someone else's!

Some advantages:

- You can be honest about the bride's dress. No one knows you from Adam.

- You don't have to buy a present.
- You can lie outrageously about yourself in the line-up.
- In their keenness to make this their daughter's perfect day, the bride's parents will probably ask for an extra seat for you at the wedding breakfast. There's bound to be a no-show anyway – though prepare to find yourself next to Great-Aunty Ethel.
- You can leave as soon as you like, without having to suffer 'YMCA', 'I Will Survive' and the like. Alternatively, stay till the bitter end and *express yourself through the medium of dance*.
- You will provide years of entertainment for the happy couple, who, every time they look at the wedding photos, will fail to agree on whether you were 'bride' or 'groom'.

Have your fortune told

Fly over your house

Need a new perspective on things? Well, why not get a bird's-eye view of your life – by flying over your own home?

Never knew your house looked that big or small? That the stripes on number 5's lawn were so much better than your own? That six doors down has a swimming pool as well as a Maserati? That the house at the end of the road is having a party, and most of the neighbours appear to be there? Never mind the neighbours, what about the park and the open fields you had no idea were only seven streets away?

Other advantages:

- Going up in a hot-air balloon or microlight is great fun . . . unless you're scared of a) heights, b) flying.

Like an arachnophobe *handling a tarantula*, though, why not take the chance to overcome your fears?

- You can impress and irritate the neighbours, as you fly to and fro in your helicopter – especially if you can land it in your back garden.
- Hang-gliding allows you to fly as well as see like a bird – but do be careful of phone lines, pylons and the like. A close-up view of your missing roof tiles isn't what we're aiming for here.

Complete *The Times* cryptic crossword

Serenade somebody

Would your loved one fall for the sound of your voice? Give it a go – it will wake up the neighbours at any rate, so you'll **become a part of your local community** without even trying. Really belt it out, the better to demonstrate your devotion.

If it turns out your romantic warbling is more nails-scratching-a-blackboard than up to scratch, why not practise at a karaoke night? No worries if the audience think you're flat as a pancake and the microphone is squeaking hideously – just keep crooning until you hear the cries of 'Crap!' It's a tried-and-tested way to build up confidence for that soulful serenade . . . if you survive the beer mats thrown at you. Come on, it can't be said that you've never done karaoke, can it?

Good karaoke choices:

• Most Abba and Frank Sinatra hits.

Bad karaoke choices:

• 'Bohemian Rhapsody' by Queen.
• 'If You're Not The One' by Daniel Bedingfield (too many squeaky notes).

Karaoke clichés:

• 'Delilah'; 'My Way'.

Avoid turning into your mother or father

This is to be done *after* you've turned forty.

Host a fancy-dress party

If you never had one when you were a kid, why not have one now? Masked ball; Gangster and Moll; Pink and Pinstripe; Pyjama Party; Red, White and Blue; Hawaiian Beach Party; Dare to Bare – the possibilities for making your friends look very silly are endless, really. Just get on with it before you look like you're hosting the annual convention of pantomime dames.

Spend the night in police cells

When, in x years' time, the grandchildren gather round you and ask, with innocent, shining eyes: 'What's the worst thing you *ever* did?' do you really want to disappoint them with the answer, 'I once took a library book back two weeks late'? Of course not. So act now to ensure you have some truly terrible delinquent tales to make their hair stand on end. Don't do it after forty: your relations will deduce you're suffering from early senile dementia and have you locked up in a residential home before you have the opportunity to cause any more damage or start getting your bits out in public.

One word of warning: don't do anything *too* criminal. One night in police cells may be construed as a reckless achievement; thirty years behind bars is well beyond the call of duty.

Go to a nudist beach

All of us are born naked. Now, understandably you want to put clothes on to keep warm or to protect the more sensitive parts of the anatomy, but why are we so fussed by the idea of a nude body? Yeah, yeah, we know about Adam and Eve wearing fig leaves. Now get your clothes off.

Reasons to go nude include:

- You can ditch your copy of *What Not to Wear*.
- No more worries about tan marks.
- Swimming naked feels fantastic (incidentally the

'skinny' in 'skinny-dipping' derives from 'skin' not 'thin').

- No more struggling to hold your beach towel up as you negotiate getting your clothes off and your swimwear on.
- You'll make more vitamin D.
- You can ogle the talent from behind your beach read (not good etiquette, but hey).
- You can get back to nature and generally hang loose.

Reasons not to go nude:

- You might get goose bumps.
- You might burn your nipples or backside.
- You have to keep an extra eye on sand crabs, jellyfish and the like.
- You need to keep up with this month's waxing style.
- You'll find the sand gets where the sun doesn't shine.
- You'll realize what you might look like at sixty.

Befriend a down-and-out

Simply giving a handful of change to the local tramp doesn't count. Give them your attention, instead – mull over the meaning of life and put the world to rights. Hunker down and have a conversation with the person you normally cross the road to avoid: find out their life story,* share ruminations on the current political landscape, exchange views and generally offer them the overflowing cup of friendship rather than the price of a cup of tea. Don't be too noble about this, either – this isn't about patronizing the poor. In fact, you may be surprised at the pleasures and insights such conversations provide. For you, that is.

* If said life story is a hair-raising rollercoaster ride of passion, intrigue, family heartache and unforgettable pain, you may wish to *get creative* and seal a publishing deal within an hour of jotting down all the salient details. Whether your new friend is in on the deal or not is down to your generous nature (or otherwise).

Plant a tree

By forty you will have breathed in a lot of oxygen and used a lot of paper. Therefore, it's high time to give the plant world something back. If everyone planted a tree it would go a long way towards preventing deforestation and would give the animals and some tribal peoples back their homes. Additionally, a healthy tree will live a lot longer than you – in fact the giant Californian redwoods are the oldest living things on earth. Just think, if you were to carve your initials on your tree, it's just possible that someone might read them hundreds of years from now. That's quite something, isn't it? Go dig out your spade.

Play topless darts

First things first: the point of the game is not to win. The more competitive among you may find this idea hard to grasp at first, but once you're surrounded by your bare-chested fellow players (of both genders), you'll soon get to grips with the situation.

How to get the game going:

- Never organize a game of topless darts by pre-planning. Even an innocent announcement at the start of an evening ('Hey! Let's all play topless darts tonight!') can be construed as premeditated lechery. Instead, gently coax people on side with copious amounts of alcohol.

- If you're not blessed with a freak heatwave, fortuitously timed to coincide with said game of topless darts, crank up that central heating and install blow heaters. When strip comes to shove, they'll be disrobing faster than you can say, 'Who's brave enough to go first?' Join 'em – and quick.
- For added hilarity, add a photo to the centre of the dartboard. Tailor the image to your crew. Teachers love a politician. Coppers dig a serial killer. Bitchy women savour an ostracized former member of their clique. Guys go for José Mourinho. And everyone delights in George W. Bush.

Do a tequila slammer

Have a holiday romance

No doubt you've already had a foreign fling at some point in your life: perhaps with that shy German pen pal from your schooldays, or during that not-for-the-faint-hearted 18-30 holiday (what goes on tour stays on tour, but you definitely took home more than a few memorable moments from that particular trip). You'll already know that exotic encounters are well worth the cost of the plane ticket. However, as *Shirley Valentine* attests, it's never too late to savour those stirrings in your loins as a scantily clad stranger saunters by on the beach. Make the most of being away from home: ambush that sexy señor or señorita and, as Ricky Martin would advise, live *la vida loca*. Hot days and hotter nights make for a temperature-rising rapport. Why not brush up on your language skills by seducing someone fluent in the native tongue? Familiarity breeds contempt, but unfamiliarity breeds like rabbits. Enjoy!

Stand on the Equator

There are certain things you need to take a stand on in life, and one of these is the Equator. This imaginary line runs through thirteen countries, and is almost 25,000 miles long. Plenty of standing room, then. Reasons to visit the Equator include:

- You can cross the line. No, this doesn't mean turning forty – it means being initiated into The Solemn Mysteries of the Ancient Order of the Deep as you sail across the Equator. Be aware, the Equator runs across more sea than land.
- The sun is more likely to be overhead, although tropical regions very close to the Equator are wet all year round – so take your brolly. Incidentally, the highest point on the Equator (in Ecuador) is above the snowline, so leave your Manolos behind.
- You weigh less at the Equator than you do at the North Pole. Definitely worth a trip!
- You can have one foot on either side of the world, or one in each hemisphere, if you prefer.

Make friends with your fellow commuters

Every day of the working week, you do the same journey into work. You probably share that journey with the same people every day, too. Take a look at them. That man with the long nose who's always doing Sudoku puzzles. That woman who was pregnant a while back and has since looked really tired. The girl who does her make-up with an unfeasibly steady hand. The boy who listens to his iPod at full volume. Why not say hi? Go on – they might think you're strange, but you're just being friendly. Dare yourself. Shake hands with everyone. With the whole train carriage. With the whole bus! Take it a step further. Bring in muffins, home-baked of course. Give them out, as a wholesome treat. Smile at people, nod. Make eye contact. Some will not be interested. Others, well, they might just smile back. Make acquaintances. Make friends. It makes the journey fly by.

Learn a new craft

Do you regret never paying attention during woodwork, art or pottery lessons at school? Well, now is the time to start learning a new craft – it may introduce you to a new you, and uncover hidden talents you never thought you had.

Reasons to give it a whirl:

- It will keep your mind and hands active.
- You'll meet new friends, even meet new lovers – everyone remembers the pottery scene in *Ghost*.
- It could be a useful supplement to your income – your hand-embroidered tops could find their way on to eBay.
- You can save a fortune on presents by giving your latest macramé marvels to (good) friends at Christmas.
- You can get revenge on crafty relations. They gave you handmade cards instead of buying real ones – now you can send your own versions back!
- It can be cool – everyone knows knitting is the new rock 'n' roll.
- You can de-stress: smacking something hard with a hammer can be very relaxing.

Fall in love

Birds do it, bees do it, so why do educated humans make such a pig's ear of it? If you are immune to falling in love, look out for the following signs:

♥ your heart flutters ♥ your knees tremble ♥ your eyes shine ♥ you can't breathe ♥ you can't stop looking at them even when you're trying not to ♥ you make excuses to be near them ♥ you want to introduce them to all your mates – and your parents ♥ you hang on their every word ♥ often you don't need to talk at all ♥ you feel comfortable holding hands ♥ you can't take your hands off them ♥ you laugh a lot ♥ you look beautiful ♥ you buy each other silly presents ♥ you can't eat – you get thinner ♥ you eat ice cream and doughnuts together – you get fatter ♥ you spend all day in bed together ♥

you can't sleep at night ❤ you choose baby names for a laugh ❤ you realize spending a month's salary on a ring would be the least you could do for this person ❤ you don't want to be with anyone else ever again (so you think!).

Of course, you're never too old to fall in love, but if you haven't done it by the time you're forty you should probably be asking yourself what you're waiting for. There are 6.5 billion people on this planet – surely one of them will make your heart skip a beat?

Answer the phone for a whole day using a kazoo

Behave inappropriately somewhere posh

Ever since you had to help out, aged eight, at your cousin's wedding – trussed up in a little sailor suit or awash with pink ruffles – you've nurtured this desire. How cool would it have been to have innocently eaten all the after-dinner mints ahead of time – and then thrown up over the wedding gifts? Forget the first dance: as far as you were concerned, that polished dance floor could have been your kingdom. Goddamn, you should have ruled it with an iron fist all night, throwing so many funky shapes that no one could have competed, even if they'd had a set square at their disposal.

Of course, back then you were oppressed, your social creativity stifled by the watchful and unfairly suspicious gaze of several relatives. But now . . . well, what's stopping you? Try these delinquencies on for size, and let that long-held ambition out to play. It'll thank you. Be loud, be proud, but above all, be awful.

TOP TIPS:

- Swing from a chandelier.
- Slide down the banisters in an elegant setting.
- Play hide-and-seek at midnight in a stately home.
- Turn up drunk to your annual work dinner.
- Ignore an instruction to wear black tie; go for the white-trash look instead.
- Dominate the dance floor with moves you learnt from the movie *Showgirls*.
- Start a food fight in a fancy restaurant.

Show a tourist round your city

You'll probably have done the major sights a thousand times before (what else is there to do when the in-laws come to visit?), but showing a tourist round your home town brings a fresh pair of eyes to the most familiar of landmarks and makes you appreciate what's right on your doorstep. Guide your tourist way off the beaten track, too – the impact of the grandest of cathedrals may be surpassed by the gentle delights of a hidden alleyway secreting little-known bars and shops. In researching your route, you may learn something new about your city – be it that a famous queen once slept above the chip shop; or perhaps the location of a to-die-for restaurant you never knew existed; or a handy short-cut to get to work. Make sure you also:

- Make use of the local farmers' market or craft fair.
- Complete your city's notorious pub crawl.
- Walk a route you've never taken before.
- Picnic in a beautiful green space.
- Develop a cabbie's knowledge of the back streets.

Get a star named after you

If you want to get a star named after you, it's easy. Just look on the Internet and for a small fee someone will tell you that you are now immortalized in the heavens. Be warned, however, that the International Astronomical Union disassociates itself from such practices and advises that these 'names' have no official validity whatsoever. So you're unlikely to appear on any star maps any time soon. But who cares? It's just a bit of fun, isn't it?

Of course, by forty you'll be far too old and sensible to get ripped off in such a way, and will have your eye glued to the small print instead of the night sky.

Order a martini, shaken not stirred

Perform a striptease

Go on, be a tease. A night of 'look don't touch' can be seriously erotic. You could do this for the private pleasure of your partner at home, or, if you really dare to bare, get on stage or on a table in a club. Pick your venue with care, however. While you might get away with it in Ibiza, in a classy joint you could find yourself in the arms of the bouncer.

There's no reason why guys shouldn't have a go at this, too. The dance of the tie, the shirt, socks, shoes and underpants has some catching up to do on the seven veils, but hey, what girl didn't love *The Full Monty*?

If you need to build up confidence first, why not practise at the local gym? Most places offer pole-dancing classes these days as a great way to get in shape. So then, shape up and strip off! (You could *streak at a major sporting event* or *go to a nudist beach*, too, now you're truly body confident.)

Remember, think 'tease' before 'strip'. Making your performance last is key. A hasty hurling-off of your clothes in different directions will probably see you falling over your pants and falling about laughing. Seduce the spectators slowly, instead. You never know, you might even get a good tip.

Organize a surprise birthday party for someone

. . . And keep it a secret.

Say 'Yes' to everything for a day

Go on, be nice. For one whole day if people ask you to do something, say 'YES!' Just think of the friends you'll make and how life-changing this could be.

The plus points:

- You agreed to go on a round-the-world trip with a friend for six months.
- Your boss treated you to dinner at the Wolseley for agreeing to work late.
- Serious brownie points earned for agreeing to have Mother-in-law round for Sunday lunch.
- You finally had sex for the first time in months.
- The children love you.

The minus points:

- You'll have to negotiate six months off work.
- You missed your anniversary meal because you couldn't say no to dinner with your boss.
- Mother-in-law is coming for Sunday lunch.
- Sex with the post boy was not really what you had in mind.
- You have ten children coming for a sleepover.

Lay down your voice in a professional recording studio

Have a ruthless clear-out of your belongings

It's never been more fashionable to cast off the old. According to some TV programmes, there's a hoard of potential cash in every attic, while a couple of good sales in an eBay auction is enough to send anyone into a clear-out frenzy, to say nothing of the influence of feng shui, minimalist designers and house doctors. Who wants to descend into middle age surrounded by the sad mementoes of your lost youth, Miss Havisham-style? Wipe the slate (and the attic) clean and advance fearlessly into the future, unencumbered by forty years' worth of junk.

Reasons to have a clear-out:

- It's cathartic.
- You'll find your missing socks.
- You can read old correspondence/look at old photographs.
- Your old rubbish might do surprisingly well in a boot sale or on eBay.
- Your house will seem bigger.
- You can *give to charity*.
- You can buy lots of new stuff.

See a sunrise

It has to be done at least once, doesn't it? To stay up all night you can try:

- playing computer games.
- reading a book.
- all-night partying.
- going to a ball or function where breakfast is served at 5 a.m.
- *having a baby*.
- working shifts.
- developing insomnia.
- sleeping all day.
- heading to somewhere like Norway or Alaska in summer, for a taste of perpetual daylight.

If you're so over all that, why not see a fantastic sunset instead, like those found in Hawaii, Thailand, Key West or San Francisco? Or head to the far north to catch the last sunset of summer (the sun then dips below the horizon until January). Time to catch up on some sleep then.

Give to charity

You've lived nearly forty years on this planet, in this society. Isn't now the time to give something back, to help others who have not been quite as fortunate as you? Whether your chosen charity focuses on homelessness, children or even meerkats, the important thing is to take some action. *Stand up for what you believe in*. Donate some of your hard-earned (or easily gained) cash to a worthy cause. No matter if you buy a pink ribbon for breast cancer or donate a substantial sum to Save The Whales, you are still doing your bit.

Remember, it's easy to make a buck, but a lot harder to make a difference. So why not take part in a charity fund-raising event? You could organize a sale or auction. Or go on a sponsored walk, run, swim, sleep or bicycle ride. Or jump out of an aeroplane (thereby *pushing yourself to the limits of your physical endurance*). Perhaps do something silly, like sitting in a bath of blancmange or baked beans for a day. You might feel a bit foolish, but the funds you raise will make it well worthwhile.

Visit a beauty salon

Are you taking good care of yourself or do you need a little pampering? If you have a problem with body hair, breakouts, cracked heels and chipped nails – get thee to a beauty salon. And yes, that includes you, men. If you haven't learned to groom yourself by now, someone had better do it for you. Remember, some things are best left to the professionals – like Brazilians.

By forty you should be body confident. But whether you're brashly *going to a nudist beach* or are, in fact, sadly noting signs of wear and tear, nothing beats the benefits of a full-body massage. Surrender yourself to the skill of your masseuse's hands: it's like you've died and gone to heaven, only without *looking death in the face*. Facials, manicures, pedicures, body wraps – each treatment will leave you looking and feeling a million dollars, without costing anywhere near as much. The indulgence is well worth it. To really up the ante, book yourself a weekend away at a spa, and perhaps *visit hot springs* while you're at it. Spoil yourself silly.

Gamble

Life is all about risk-taking. Why not have a little wager on the way? It's never been easier to gamble than it is today, with scratchcards and lottery tickets on sale alongside the bread and milk, and online poker sites just a click away. You don't even need to set foot in a smoky bookies, instead place your bets from the comfort of your own home. So whether you fancy a flutter on the gee-gees, the dogs, the footie or perhaps the latest reality-TV eviction, bite the bullet and put your money where your mouth is. You never know – Lady Luck might just be on your side. If you get a taste for it, cruise to a casino and try to build a fortune, Las Vegas-style. While you're there, *get married (for 48 hours)* and see if that winning streak extends to the world of romance. For money isn't everything. Gamble in life, too. *Go on a blind date*. Dare to *fall in love*. *Start your own business*. Live on the edge.

Push yourself to the limits of your physical endurance

When was the last time you really pushed yourself physically? When you tramped the length and breadth of the shopping centre in search of shoes? Or maybe when, having propped up the bar all evening in Herculean fashion, you won out in the valiant struggle to walk in a straight line to the door.

Come on, we are talking about really pushing yourself. About going through the pain barrier, the wall. No more being a couch potato. Get off the sofa and up a mountain instead!

TOP TIPS:

- Climb something – like Snowdon (there's a train back, after all). Then tackle Kilimanjaro or Everest.
- Ski down a double-black run – slightly easier than climbing up one, as long as you can stop.
- Jump out of an aeroplane – ideally with a parachute, unless you're a real daredevil.
- Bungee jump – become a human yo-yo to experience the ups and downs of life.
- Train for a marathon.
- Trek across a desert.
- Join a football team.
- Stick with your gym membership for a year – your waist will be smaller and so will your wasted cash.

Make a fashion faux pas

It's highly unlikely that you'll have lived nearly four decades without making a single fashion faux pas, for the simple reason that at least one of those decades will have long since gone out of fashion. The good news is that your wardrobe will soon be retro and cool again (watch out for teenagers raiding it for authentic vintage items).

It's great to make a fashion faux pas before you're forty. At this age, you're still experimenting, and you're permitted the odd mistake. After forty, however, such errors will simply be a reflection that you have allowed age to overtake your passion for fashion – a sign that you're now more vague than vogue. So enjoy these last few years of freedom and flirt with every fad that hits the high street. If you find yourself in the same clothes as your children, it's a faux pas (unless they're dressing up in yours). If it's an outfit that *stops the traffic*, it may still be a faux pas, but you'll have achieved every fashionista's fantasy of getting noticed (so show-stopping hats off to you). Try neon colours, sheer fabrics, revealing cuts and clinging clothes . . . while you still can.

Look death in the face

As we approach the big 4-0, it's only the brave or the foolish who don't feel the odd tremor of concern regarding their own mortality. The only way to beat it is to look death in the face (all right, so eating healthily and fitting in some regular exercise also have advocates, but this is the alternative). It's easier than you might think, and thankfully requires no ab crunches.

First, think about what will happen after you go. How would you like to be remembered? More realistically, how will you actually be remembered? Write your will. Decide on your epitaph and, if you're in the public eye (which you will be, of course, having *sold your story to the tabloids*), consider where that life-size bronze statue of you would be best positioned in your home town.

Undoubtedly, you will have been affected by death at some point in your life. So perhaps you have already, unwittingly, looked death in the face. Were you with someone when they passed away? Have you ever seen an open casket at a funeral? If you're a mortician or a homicide detective, you'll have seen more dead bodies than you care to remember. For the rest of us, it's a unique experience. Explore how it makes you feel. Experience grief, wonder, horror, fascination. Fear. Denial. Peace.

Wear a miniskirt

Win a pub quiz

It may be naff, but it's not for fools and it's not for laughs. To win a pub quiz – like the pub itself, a largely British phenomenon – you will need a surprisingly good general knowledge (or teammates with such, so round them up), as well as the stamina for several pints.

Now the more you enter said quizzes, the more you'll get an idea of what's needed. You can also buy quiz books, or research typical questions on many Internet sites. But of course the most difficult challenge posed all night is having to come up with a quality team name. If it gets a laugh every time the scores of each round are read out, the real result won't matter.

Act out a sexual fantasy

Have you ever thought how much your sex life might improve if you could do what you fantasize about for real? You only have one life, you know, and it's best to try these things before you're too far past your (sexual) peak.

Do act on such fantasies as:

- Wanting an audience (try *having sex in public*).
- Wanting to be Miss Whiplash for a night – make your partner beg for mercy.
- Wanting to play the innocent – be mastered.
- Wanting to make love in the rain.

Be cautious about:

- Having a threesome (someone always feels left out).

Best not to act on:

- Pouncing on a stranger on a train.
- Sleeping with your boss, or your best friend's partner (unless you're intent on *dating someone unsuitable*).
- Meeting a stranger in the middle of the night.
- Getting kidnapped.

Send a message in a bottle

Host Christmas for your family

Forget the family rows for the moment. The fussy eaters, the ungrateful kids, the unnecessary expense and all the fuss. Think of the occasion, instead: this is perhaps the one time of year when all the family is together (for better or worse). Wouldn't it be great to be at the heart of all that – the provider of home, hearth, and good cheer, the merry-maker who makes everyone merry with a good stock of festive spirits? If not for any other reason, it will spare the chump who usually hosts it one year of tearing their hair out. Their salon will thank you, as will they (preferably with an over-generous gift).

Hosting Christmas is a pretty grown-up affair and you really should be a pro at it by the time you're forty. There's a lot to think about – and it goes beyond circling the best programmes to watch in the TV guide.

TOP TIPS:

- Start planning early. July should do it.
- Delegate. You can't possibly be expected to manage everything, so allocate jobs to others. If done wisely, you'll be left with the telly guide circling and not a lot else.
- Buy in lots of booze. If the turkey goes tits up, everyone will be too far gone to notice.

Write in the sand

Complete a first-aid course

Whether you aspire to be a George Clooney-alike in his infamous *ER* role, or love the idea of playing nurse, completing a first-aid course is the first step in realizing those dreams. And not only will you be medically proficient when *acting out that* (doctors-and-nurses) *sexual fantasy*, you'll actually be able to assist people in their hour of need. That's pretty amazing. If someone starts choking in a restaurant, you can leap to their aid. If your partner is struck down by a freak skin condition, you can lovingly bandage their weeping sores (possibly before *having a messy break-up*, if the condition is truly minging). If you have the misfortune to be caught up in a terrorist attack, you'll be able to provide the kind of hands-on help that will make a real difference. So what are you waiting for? Equip yourself with the skills to save lives. You never know when your knowledge could be called upon, and when knowing what to do in an emergency will be the difference between life and death.

Attend a launch party

There are fewer things more exciting in life than being at a birth. For obvious reasons, maternity wards tend to object to random strangers lingering in their vicinity, so you have to get your kicks elsewhere. Being at the birth of a new age can be just as gratifying. At launch parties, whatever is being launched will be described as 'ushering in a new age of . . .' (literature/aerodynamics/kitchen technology – you fill in the blank). As this announcement is made, applaud lightly and nod sagely, as if you know what's going on. For launch parties are incredibly easy to gatecrash. Nine times out of ten the person standing next to you clutching their glass of warm white wine and a cheesy nibble is also a stranger to the gathering. This is why no one will object if you scoff the entire buffet – and why launch parties are the perfect locations for scamming free nosh and booze.

Attend a launch for a:

- Book (literary types – lots of liquor about).
- Company (stingy spread – they've only got their start-up capital to play with, and it's all been spent on an Ikea-furnished office).
- Invention (mad scientists galore – work the room quickly and efficiently, to avoid getting trapped in a conversation about astrophysics).
- Ship (don't be embittered by the waste of champagne).

See creatures in their natural habitat

In the age of David Attenborough documentaries and the Discovery Channel, there's really no excuse not to have done this. But why should Sir Dave have all the fun? See the animal kingdom first-hand and with your own two eyes. Get near enough to touch. The telly can't communicate the smells and senses of being up close and personal with these creatures. A zoo puts them out of context (and into captivity). See them in their natural habitat to appreciate fully their beauty, splendour and magnificence.

TOP TIPS:

- Snorkel or dive to see fish.
- Visit a nature reserve.
- Go on safari.
- While *travelling to every continent*, stop off in Antarctica and take in the penguin parade.
- Swim with dolphins.

Go to a funfair and act like a kid all day

Remember when seeing that Big Wheel on the horizon excited you so much you couldn't sleep? It was all lit up with the promise of candyfloss and thrills, the music of the merry-go-round carrying on the wind; you could almost taste the hot dogs as you tossed and turned in your bed, desperately wanting to join in the fun. Well, next time the funfair comes to town, don't miss out. Get yourself along there early, so you can get on all the rides. Scream the house down on the Big Dipper, and scare yourself silly on the Ghost Train. Take in the view from the top of that Big Wheel – can you see your house? Lose your tummy on the Pirates' Ship. Eat funfair food with relish, and get your teeth stuck into a toffee apple or two (in a few years' time, after all, you won't be able to get them out again). Buy yourself a massive candyfloss, and care not a jot when you get it all over your face and fingers. Lick it off with enthusiasm. Best of all, bag yourself a bear from the cuddly-toy range of prizes and carry it home on the bus with pride.

Start your own business

Have you ever wanted to be your own boss? To have a working life dictated by, well, nobody other than yourself? Perhaps you've nurtured a dream of being a freelancer in your chosen industry, or of jacking in the career and taking up landscape gardening, jewellery making, or even wild-boar hunting instead? Has *taking an evening class* revealed new ways of making a living? Well, now's the time to make your move. Not after forty, when the aches and pains of your body subtly hint that private health insurance is worth its weight in gold, and pension schemes seem pivotal. Do it now. *Tell your boss where to shove their job* (or not, if you need the contacts for your start-up), prepare yourself for a lot of hard work, and throw yourself into it with gusto. It's one of the most rewarding – and challenging – things you can do. Something akin to *having a baby*. Just think: never again will you worry about being in on time. You can delegate all the jobs you don't like (though maybe not at first). If you work late, it's your own money you're making. And you can pay yourself the biggest Christmas bonus you can afford . . .

Spend a week dedicating yourself to good deeds

It doesn't take much to help others. Offering a lift here, picking up a few groceries there, helping a blind man across the road or a mother with a pram up the stairs. The small things count for a lot in life.

Try dedicating yourself to good works for one week and see how you get on. You never know, you might find yourself doing something you would be genuinely glad to do on a regular basis.

TOP TIPS:

- Help in a hospital or charity shop.
- Offer your skills — such as playing the piano, hairdressing or giving manicures and pedicures — at an old people's home. Or just go there to chat or to listen.
- Help someone with their gardening and odd jobs.
- Offer to babysit for someone whom you know needs a break.
- Do someone's shopping for them.